Duncan M Simpson

stayed in his first youth hostel more than 30 years ago and on that first night never thought he would spend most of his working life, employed by the Youth Hostels Association.

He lives in Derbyshire on the edge of the Peak District National Park. He gave up having a car more than ten years ago and walks when he can, bikes or uses public transport. When he has to, he hires a car.

He loves words, sentences and stories. He reads and writes because he can't help it. He has written since he first read *Swallows and Amazons* and realised that words have a power to carry us into a different world.

He is lucky enough now to be able to write full time and to work on projects that engross him. He writes about youth hostels, their history and the people and ideas behind them.

He worked in youth hostels all over England and Wales, and at the association's national office as head of communications and corporate affairs for 15 years, witnessing first hand years of change and the aftermath of the foot and mouth outbreak on one of Britain's foremost and best loved charities.

RICHARD SCHIRRMANN

The man who invented youth hostels

RICHARD SCHIRRMANN

The man who invented youth hostels

Duncan M Simpson

Contents

Illustrations

Preface to the Second Edition

At the end of my research, when I came to write *Open to All – how youth hostels changed the world*, the story of Richard Schirrmann would not fit. Early readers commented that the story was too much and that it would work better on its own. So I took what I had written and turned it into its own small book.

With no publisher for either book I considered publishing the book independently of any publishing house. It seemed like a big step and a short book on Richard Schirrmann made an ideal experiment. I could test the systems and see how 'indie' publishing might work for me, without risking all the work of a bigger book. I took the story of Richard Schirrmann and turned it into a small book.

The experiment worked but the book had some weaknesses and

some glaring faults when it was done. That's how experiments go. The errors and mistakes were largely in the design and layout. My publishing software had no facility for headers. Placing images distorted the text.

After two years, wanting to make the book more widely available I've taken the chance to correct those errors and make available a second edition. I've taken the chance to tidy some minor stylistic, typographic and grammatical errors too. Print-on-demand makes it possible to produce a second edition with little cost.

For owners of the first edition, do not worry. The text of your edition is largely the same as the text of this edition and I would not recommend spending your hard earned cash on this edition. But if you didn't have the previous edition, this is the one for you.

Duncan M Simpson
Derbyshire, August 2017

Note: In 2020 new information came to light regarding the Nazi take-over of youth hostels in Germany and this edition has been revised to take note of that.

Introduction

Youth hostels cover the world. You can find them in cities, in the countryside and beside the sea, on every continent of the world. Official and unofficial, hostels, backpackers, bunkhouses, call them what you will, they've conquered the world. If you've never stayed in one, youth hostels offer something special, best described as a relaxed and informal communal atmosphere. They're focused on young people but everyone is welcome and people from all walks of life can mix freely in a youth hostel.

Youth hostels owe their existence to one man. Richard Schirrmann, a school teacher in Germany, invented them. Caught in a thunderstorm when walking with his pupils in 1909, they sheltered in a school. While his pupils slept, Richard Schirrmann lay awake, listening to the storm. He dreamed of a chain of simple places, spreading across the countryside, where young people might stay. Travelling between these youth hostels, children would be out in the fresh air. They would walk, exercise and stretch their limbs. Travel and being close to nature would make them better people.

Schirrmann's story is important. Just as the parent's genes are carried in a child, youth hostels carry some of the traits of the man who invented them. They are romantic and down to earth, just as Schirrmann was. Practical and impractical at the same time.

Schirrmann is also inspiring because, in today's world, he is different. From a humble background, he developed an idea which spread around the world and which has blossomed into many different guises. But he took very little financial reward from his invention. He never copyrighted his idea, never built it into a brand or sold it to anyone.

He was an enthusiast, a volunteer and an amateur in the best sense of the word. People like him seem to have vanished from our lives. We celebrate the success of individualism as if these are the only values worth espousing. Our heroes are entrepreneurs and buccaneering businessmen.

Richard Schirrmann shows that there are other ways of making a difference in the world.

Duncan M Simpson
Derbyshire, October 2015

Down to Earth

When Richard Schirrmann moved to Altena, a small town surrounded by the Sauerland's wooded hills, in 1903, life for the newly married 29-year-old teacher was full of promise. The Sauerland is an outdoor paradise for those escaping the industrial cities of the Ruhr. In summer there is walking and in winter skiing.

"Heavens," he wrote. "What a change. From the fumes, dust, and reeking air to a clean little town ringed about with wooded hills."

Tall, slim, long-legged and with an athletic frame, Schirrmann was a strong walker and natural athlete. He could, a biographer claimed, walk 45 miles in a day. He spoke "a vivid, pithy German, full of unusual turns of phrase, and with an infectious enthusiasm which made his whole face light up".

In Altena he joined the local walking club, teaming up with working parties to mark long distance paths through the Sauerland with coloured paint, splashed on tree trunks or stones. He preferred solitary walking but he led tours for an Altena group of the club.

He also enjoyed walking with his pupils in the woodland and hills around the town, where they filled their lungs with clear fresh air, where their eyes escaped the tiny print of books to focus on space and distance, on meadow and woodland.

He believed that not only were the outdoors and fresh air good for their spirits but young children learned best in the natural world. At his previous school and at college he had begun developing ideas for a *wandernde Schule*, a wandering school.

Convinced a teacher couldn't teach just by standing in front of his pupils using only words and speech and examining them afterwards to find out what they had learned, he wanted his pupils to really learn, to feel, to understand and explore the world, to become better people.

Young children learned best out of the classroom. In the natural world, in small groups, learning together, they could really experience and understand nature and geography. Pupils and parents would remember Schirrmann fondly and they would wish that all teachers were like him.

But in the paradise of Altena, Schirrmann's enthusiasm rapidly ran into disappointment. He and his recently married wife discovered they had little in common and very different tastes. His trusting, optimistic nature had brought him into difficulties it would be hard to escape. Schirrmann described the marriage as one made out of pity and it caused unhappiness, leading to separation, and finally divorce, twenty-six years later.

Compounding his predicament, the head teacher of his new

school banned Schirrmann from taking the children out of school during school time. But Schirrmann was a rebellious, determined man. He took them instead on free afternoons and weekends, going further and further afield. When he wanted to take a longer trip, in the school holidays, going out for several days, his headmaster quoted regulations, which had already been broken, and refused permission to the walking mad teacher. Aged 29 his plans and dreams had run into the ground.

Schirrmann was born in 1874 in Grunenfeld, East Prussia, now Gronówko in Poland, where his father taught at a small school and kept cows, pigs, bees and hens on a small holding to supplement his pay.

The young Schirrmann's childhood was idyllic. He helped out with the animals, and roamed the surrounding countryside, in his bare feet, developing the strength of his walking and his love of the outdoors. From it he took his lifelong love of walking but also a practical, earthy approach. His father taught him until he was old enough for a larger school.

A childhood like his was becoming increasingly rare. More and more children were growing up in towns and cities, among mines, factories and cramped houses, more and more distant from the natural world.

Schirrmann, intent on being a teacher like his father and grandfather before him, went from school to teacher training college in 1891. Here he opened his eyes to an unexpectedly new way of teaching, one that fitted his nature and would stick with him for the rest of his life. Every year at Whitsuntide the geography tutor took his students on a walking tour, so that they could study landscape and geology by walking among hills, fields and woods. Touching rocks and holding stones in their hands they learned better than was possible in any lecture hall or classroom. Watching how a river moves through hills, sculpting a valley, is a much better way of learning than any book offers.

"This single walking tour assumed such importance in our life as eighteen year-olds, that we dreamed of it for a year beforehand and talked about it for years afterwards," Schirrmann remembered.

The tour at Whitsuntide was a revelation. "I still remember how we gazed at the first mountains, felt and tapped the first rock faces to see whether they were made or real stone or not... We saw lightening and rain clouds below us, looked down through gaps in the clouds on the great and yet so small world lying far, far below us…"

After the joy and freedom of the great outdoors the atmosphere of college when they returned was cramped, the curriculum limited and the teaching poor. Following discontent, and a demonstration at the college, the authorities picked on Schirrmann as the ringleader of the rebels, wrongly it was claimed, and expelled him.

Fortunately for the young man a sympathetic tutor found a job for him; tutoring the children of a wealthy family. Out of a formal school Schirrmann could try teaching the way he had learned from his geography tutor. He took his new pupils out in the family carriage, enjoying teaching them in the real world in an easy going, relaxed manner, beginning to show an attitude to younger people that was open and encouraging, rather than stiff and autocratic.

Despite the break in his training he took the exams for his teacher's diploma. He passed, and in May 1895 took up teaching in a two-class primary school in Masuria, Prussia, now Poland.

Most of his pupils spoke a dialect unfamiliar to Schirrmann. He resorted to teaching them in his practical way. He took them roaming the countryside on foot, on bicycle and, in winter, on skates, playing games, singing songs and developing his new method of learning in the natural world. It was, he said, a real paradise for education.

Schirrmann was an ambitious man. Unlike his father, he was not content to stay in one place, teaching and tending a smallholding. In 1901 he moved to a school at Gelsenkirchen in a coal mining district of the Ruhr. The horror of the dirty industrial town, the air thick with fumes and dust from the surrounding mines and factories, horrified him. The children, he recalled, never heard birdsong, never saw a green field. He recoiled from the dirt and misery. Once again he took his young pupils on excursions into the nearby hills, continuing his wandering school.

"Their cheeks glow, their bare arms grow tanned," he exulted. The children, experiencing the countryside, its meadows, fields, ponds and streams for the first time, were unlikely to forget the experience. One boy, seeing fish swim in a stream, exclaimed with awe, "…fish, real, genuine, living fish". Their reaction and excitement convinced Schirrmann that this was the right way of teaching, that the outdoors was good for the physical, mental and spiritual well-being of his pupils.

Others were thinking the same and not just for children. Many people were beginning to believe that being outdoors, walking in the fresh air was good for everyone. The ideas of romanticism, that people belonged in the natural world and that they could be improved and bettered by being in that natural world, were spreading and the numbers thinking like that rising.

In Austria, the *Natuurfreunde*, Friends of Nature, set out in 1897, as part of the social democratic movement, to open the outdoors for ordinary people so that they could get closer to nature through walking and exploring. They opened chalets and accommodation, believing that fresh air improved people's lives.

In 1903 when he transferred to Altena with his new wife, Schirrmann must have been surprised when his head teacher opposed his plans. With other groups and movements springing up to encourage young people into the outdoors, he must have believed that the rest of society was moving in the direction he had chosen. Except, his head teacher.

Determined, and undeterred Schirrmann applied for a transfer to another school in the town, with a headmaster more sympathetic to his ideas. At the new school he arranged more walking tours. He kept the groups small so that conversation, and chatter didn't blind the children to their surroundings and swamp their senses.

His pupils loved the variety, and excitement their teacher brought to the school. A grateful pupil recalled "Schirrmann never tired of giving his pupils new experiences. When we came home again we couldn't stop talking about the trip…"

He also ran accommodation for walkers and hikers. For a short time he had been the warden at a scholars' and students' hostel in Altena. Guido Rotter, a factory owner, also a keen climber and walker, had set up a network of hostels in private homes, in schools and inns so that male students and secondary school pupils could escape into the country.

Another group had a wider impact on Schirrmann and others like him in Germany as the twentieth century began. Senior pupils from a school in Berlin began making trips on foot though the countryside, carrying their own provisions, sleeping in barns or the open air. The practice of wandering spread to Berlin University, and in 1901 the first group of *Wandervogel*, wandering birds, established itself there. Young people in the group set their own agenda without adults. They began a genuine youth movement of their own, long before the wider youth revolutions of beatniks and hippies.

The *Wandervogel* openly rebelled against the contemporary life of Germany. They dressed casually in open necked shirts, and shorts, abandoning formal traditional walking clothes. They were vehemently teetotal and anti-smoking. Sleeping in the outdoors, singing folk songs as they walked with guitars and flags, their enthusiastic rebelliousness exploded through Germany.

Theirs was a back-to-nature movement focused on simplicity and revolt against established traditions. They helped on farms in exchange for somewhere to stay and built or adapted from existing buildings their own places to stay. At first only boys took part but, later, girls joined too.

The movement caught Schirrmann's imagination. At his new school he improvised a hostel for the *Wandervogel* in the summer holidays of 1907. Each night Schirrmann, helped by the school caretaker and his wife, pushed away the desks, and benches. They laid out straw sacks for beds and in the morning returned the room to use as a classroom with the desks and benches back in place. Some local people and teachers opposed his use of the classroom but he obstinately persisted.

RICHARD SCHIRRMANN

Whatever unhappiness his married life had caused, at his new school he was happy and busy with the children he taught, with his walking and club friends, and at night offering a place to stay for the youthful rebels wandering the countryside, talking with them as they took their own steps to create a better life.

On 26 August 1909, while on a walking tour from Altena with pupils, a violent storm further fired his imagination. When accommodation he had arranged for the night fell through, Schirrmann headed with his group to the small town of Bröl, where the school teacher let them use a class room to shelter for the night.

"The storm raged through the whole night with thunder and lightning, high wind, cloudbursts and hail, as if the end of the world had come…" While his pupils slept Schirrmann lay awake. "I thought to myself that the schools throughout Germany could very well be used to provide accommodation during the holidays… villages in good walking country could have a friendly 'youth hostel', situated a day's walk from each other, to welcome all young Germans who enjoyed walking…"

1 Richard Schirrmann

The Rising Generation

Back home, Schirrmann set out his vision. He wrote a pamphlet 'Hiking for young people and the benefits it can bring' and a year later wrote an article proposing youth hostels. He argued that *Wandervogel*, young adults, and walkers like himself could sleep rough in fields and woods, or in barns. Younger children needed more reliable shelter. They needed somewhere to sleep and to prepare meals. They also needed something more communal, where they could make friends and have fun together.

Schirrmann's article, entitled 'Elementary School Children's Hostels', set out the case for youth hostels. They would be explicitly for young children, not young adults, to ensure that children were not ignored and left out of the burgeoning opportunities in the outdoors. Crucially Schirrmann wanted a national network of youth hostels.

His design for a hostel was rudimentary, without ornamentation. The idea was practical and inexpensive, needing only the minimum of effort and expenditure, using buildings and rooms already there. Every town and almost every village had an elementary school. They were just the right kind of places for children, as Schirrmann already knew, familiar and designed for children.

He had thought it all through enough to describe what a youth hostel would be like. Youth hostels would be in school classrooms during the holiday season. "Two classrooms will suffice," he wrote. "One for boys and one for girls. Some of the benches will be stacked up. That will make room for fifteen beds. Each bed will consist of a tightly stuffed straw sack and pillow, two sheets and a blanket. Each child will be required to keep his own sleeping place clean and tidy…The resident school caretaker's wife will provide clean sheets, for which each child will pay her 20 pfennnig."

The teacher would take advance bookings, supervise cleaning beds and rooms, take money, keep accounts and store equipment at the end of the summer season.

He sent his article to German teachers' journals but his fellow professionals dismissed his idea. They saw too many problems with combining the existing roles of teachers with the 'hostel father' Schirrmann had in mind. "My dear colleague, your article asks for the impossible: straw sacks in the school… and the teachers as 'hostel fathers'. That would set our profession back a hundred years to when we had the miserable status of caretakers."

Schirrmann stubbornly persisted, despite the rebuff, searching for support. A daily newspaper, the *Kolnische Zeitung*, published his article in 1910. The newspaper reached a much wider audience that immediately understood the significance of his plans. Those who were not professional teachers saw how his ideas would benefit young people. His plans promised to open the outdoors to young children and inspired others who responded overwhelmingly with assistance and gifts, in money and kind.

Lifted by this support Schirrmann equipped his school with beds and mattresses. Visitors came from far and wide and not just classes with teachers but students and *Wandervogel*, and not, as he had expected, just in school holidays. He, and the school caretaker and his wife, found themselves setting up the hostel at the end of every school day and clearing it away before classes could be held every morning.

Success threatened to swamp his idea. Schirrmann never anticipated how demand for youth hostels would explode, nor that his fellow teachers and authorities wouldn't co-operate to make youth hostels work. Supplementing accommodation, taking groups in holidays, wasn't enough. His idea quickly required a permanent building, open all year with staff doing no other work.

Schirrmann, eminently practical, changed his thinking. In 1912, helped by the local authority and supported by his walking club, Schirrmann transferred his hostel from the original school to the castle in the town. This castle is often called the first youth hostel. The permanence of the arrangement sets it apart from Schirrmann's first temporary hostel. He designed the youth hostel at the castle, with two dormitories but this time with massive, triple-tier bunks, a kitchen, washrooms and a shower-bath.

Schirrmann had shown his ideas to be practical, capable of change and evolution. He was not an idealist, committed irrevocably to an idea. He was willing to compromise and to adapt.

Wilhelm Münker, a member of the local walking club, had become a close friend of Schirrmann's. About the same age as Schirrmann, he was a non-smoking, teetotal, vegetarian bachelor, who had inherited a small engineering factory. Behind the scenes, with his experience of running a factory, he was a growing influence. Once the hostel transferred from the school to the castle the movement quickly grew.

In 1913, a year after the hostel moved to the castle, youth hostels had opened in 301 towns and villages. The number rose to 535 the next year. Demand soared. Schirrmann's original plan had been for youth hostels one day's walk from the next, about 30 – 35 km apart. He soon modified his plan and focused on youth hostels in places important for wanderers, including towns, cities, mountains and recreational areas.

When the first world war was over, the generation who had been *Wandervogel* before the war, now grown and mature members of society in positions of power, gave widespread support for the new youth hostels. Youth hostels became a national institution, with committees, meetings, conferences, agendas and paid regional secretaries.

A Central Committee for German Youth Hostels set up in 1919 with Schirrmann as chairman and Münker as Honorary Secretary. In a federal structure, regional bodies concerned themselves with youth hostels in their area while the national organisation looked after wider issues. The pattern of a national organisation supported by regions contributed to the strength and growth of youth hostels, allowing the maximum flexibility for local initiative within a national framework to meet rampantly rising demand.

Youth hostels recorded half a million overnight stays in 1921, and by 1924 two thousand youth hostels were open. Münker gave up his job and his home became an office for the growing organisation. Schirrmann gave up teaching and both men devoted themselves full time to youth hostels.

Youth hostels in fairytale castles, like the one at Altena, stirred and caught the imagination. They became the best kind of advertising for Schirrmann's idea. But in reality castles were impractical, awkward to run and expensive to keep. By 1926, Schirrmann and others realised that they needed youth hostels built for purpose, dedicated to being one thing, not classrooms with add-ons, not castles.

Schirrmann was adamant. "We don't want to build any gloomy medieval fortress, any miniature castles from an over-romantic age with mock turrets and lighthouse-like towers, any barracks, any sheep-pens. Buildings must be constructed to accommodate youth, the rising generation; simple and functional, light, easily ventilated, yet retaining the warmth, pleasant to live in, beautiful..."

Schirrmann and his colleagues began building brand new youth hostels with generous support from public authorities. They began a completely new field of architecture. The first city hostel in Munich opened in 1927 for up to 300 guests, with a classroom attached to each dormitory and a kitchen, where groups and classes could cook their meals. Another kitchen offered meals for sale. They developed heavy and robust equipment to stand use by lively children. In less than twenty years the concept of youth hostels had leaped from ad-hoc and temporary accommodation in classrooms to purpose-built, architect-designed youth hostels with the single simple purpose of accommodating large numbers of young people.

2.Richard Schirrmann, back row, right, in 1935

Youth and Peace

The first world war set youth hostels back. With Schirrmann in the army on the Western Front and Münker in the East, Schirrmann's father kept the hostel at Altena running. A colleague from the Sauerland Mountain Club maintained the wider organisation.

Schirrmann's experience in the trenches with the German army inspired him to dream of something better when the war was over. During Christmas 1915, in the Vosges in France, he saw German and French troops mingling through disused trenches, exchanging wine, cognac, French bread and cigarettes for Westphalian black bread, biscuits and ham.

He concluded that if "thoughtful young people of all countries could be provided with suitable meeting places where they could get to know each other" peace and friendliness could be encouraged.

RICHARD SCHIRRMANN

"That could and must be the role of our youth hostels, not only in Germany, but throughout the world building a bridge of peace from nation to nation."

After the war Schirrmann was keen to see other countries take up the idea. In Germany, they welcomed visitors from other countries. In different countries for different reasons people took up Schirrmann's idea and shaped it for their own culture or politics. A lack of ideology became an advantage.

Young people in Switzerland, without adults, set up youth hostels with an executive of six young people aged 19 – 24, mainly students, in 1924.

School children's contributions financed the first hostels in Poland in 1926 where youth hostels were part of an attempt to build a new nation.

In Holland youth hostels were a foundation, without the trappings of democracy or a federation that were so much part of their establishment in Germany.

Early in 1928, wondering whether there were youth hostels in Britain, Richard Schirrmann wrote to the Anglo German Academic Bureau. He asked if young Germans travelling to Britain would find youth hostels there.

The bureau replied on 1 May 1928 that in Britain it was unlikely "the near future will bring the establishment of youth hostels. It is not customary for young people to go on tours... English young people normally go out into the country in groups and stay at one fixed point in a camp, using their own or hired tents."

Schirrmann's correspondent in Britain was right. The Scouts, the Woodcraft Folk, the Young Communist League and others organised summer camps for young people. The Co-operative Holidays Association and the Holiday Fellowship arranged holidays, mostly based at single centres.

But less than two years later youth hostels started in Britain, in Liverpool, after a group of young people returned from Germany determined that what could be done in Germany could be done in Britain.

Along with different motivations and different cultures, youth hostel regulations were developing differently in different countries. They had various styles of membership card, different age limits, different aims and objects and varying standards of equipment. None of that was a problem until the members of each wanted to visit another country, to stay in youth hostels there. They wanted their membership cards recognized and they expected similar regulations and standards.

The benefit of establishing formal links and working together was increasingly plain. In December 1931 Schirrmann and Münker met the secretaries of the Dutch, English and Scottish associations in Hildenbach near Wunsiedel in North Eastern Bavaria, close to the Czech border. They talked about convening a conference of youth hostel organisers like themselves, to create better and more formal links. Dr HLFJ Deelen, the Dutch Secretary, a stiff, formal man with a penchant for fashionable dress and plus fours, visited the Flemish, Danish and Norwegian associations.

They responded that if Deelen organised an international conference they would attend. In August 1932 Deelen invited them all to meet in Amsterdam in October and offered hospitality for the meeting.

RICHARD SCHIRRMANN

22 representatives from 11 counties (Germany, Switzerland, Czechoslovakia, Poland, Norway, Denmark, France, England and Wales, Ireland and Belgium along with the Dutch organisers) were there. Austria, Northern Ireland and Scotland, although invited, were unable to attend. Each country had been invited to send two representatives. Schirrmann and Münker represented Germany.

Terry Trench, a founder of the Irish Association, *An Óige*, Youth, attended despite the misgivings of colleagues, who failed to see what could be gained from the meeting. 'Jack' Catchpool, first secretary of the England and Wales Association, also attended. Command of the German language was required as the meetings were held in German, and Catchpool had along with him a young German speaker, Mary Landers.

Schirrmann presided and Terry Trench recalled him coming up with the phrase *solvitur ambulando*, it is solved in walking. The phrase "would have made an excellent motto for the international organisation but it was never taken up."

On 20 October 1932 they created an association of international youth hostels. They elected Schirrmann as their president and chairman, with Deelen as secretary. The new association was first known as the *Internationale Arbeitsgemeinschaft für Jugendherbergen* (IAJH). Poland, hosting a later meeting, translated the title as the International Union of the Youth Hostels Associations. It became the International Youth Hostel Federation when an international guest membership was created in 1935. The meetings were good natured and optimistic. They agreed principles and laid foundations that would support a future boom in youth travel.

Hostels were to help young people travel freely. They were to be open to all the young people of a country. There could be no discrimination.

Young people would pay lower fees, for membership and for accommodation, and they would be given priority over other guests in the allocation of beds. Boys and girls would be accommodated in separate dormitories, one to a bed, in simple and homely accommodation.

Deelen stressed the importance of education and Münker emphasised youth hostels must cater especially for young people, in line with Schirrmann's original idea. He insisted nothing should be considered too good for young people. They were not to be treated as inferior or deserving of anything less than the best.

None of the conference's principles or conclusions were binding on the new members. Membership cards would have a uniform style and size but they couldn't agree to recognise each others' membership cards. Schirrmann and Münker with Germany's 2,000 youth hostels, many more than any of the others, could not agree reciprocal memberships until there was a more equal balance of hostels across Europe. They feared they would be swamped in their own hostels by members from beyond the borders.

They agreed they would only recognise one association from any one country. Exceptions were made for Belgium, with its two associations, and two different language groups, and for Czechoslovakia, with its German minority. The exceptions were a portent of future issues over German minorities in other European countries when the Nazis came to power in Germany.

For now, the meeting in Amsterdam had established a common way of working and common understandings of what youth hostels should be, built on Schirrmann's original idea.

3.Richard Schirrmann, centre, with Catchpool, left, and Deelen, right, at Willersley Castle, Derbyshire, in 1934

Gathering Clouds

The following year the Nazis took power in Germany. They told Schirrmann and Münker that their organisation, where all boys and girls were treated equally without discrimination, was dissolved. Youth hostels, as Schirrmann invented them, came to an end in Germany.

The Nazis incorporated youth hostels into their own youth movement; the Hitler Youth. Münker resigned but Schirrmann, naively impressed with the new movement's idealism, agreed to stay on as honorary president, a decision he would later bitterly regret. Johannes Rodatz, a young Nazi who knew nothing of youth hostels, took over. Schirrmann, still president of the international federation of youth hostels, turned his attention to youth hostels outside Germany.

Schirrmann failed to distance himself from the Nazis even when their officials in party uniforms attended the second international conference in Bad Godesberg, near Bonn, in 1933. Hitler Youth, also in uniform, made a guard of honour.

The appearance of Hitler Youth and uniforms was a shock. Despite the beginnings of discrimination in Germany under the Nazis that would result in Auschwitz other countries clung to their links with Germany and continued to make reciprocal arrangements for travel to and from Germany. Many held to a noble ideal of peace. Only one of the leading figures, Alan Fothergill, took a stand against the Nazis and resigned from the YHA of Scotland.

Youth hostels had never been militaristic. Members had no uniforms. They dressed informally, often in shorts, and respected no hierarchy. There was no military drill and no athletics, except walking and cycling. The original spirit of the *Wandervogel*, who wandered rebelliously about pre-war Germany, remained strong, adding a rich romanticism to the movement.

Two teachers from the USA, Isabel and Monroe Smith, turned up at that meeting. Isabel, an art teacher from Hartford, Connecticut, and Monroe, a widower whose first wife had died in a tragic boating accident, had met in New York while Isabel was studying there.

They married in 1929 and Monroe took a job with the Boy Scouts. Isabel believed that working with the scouts, he would be "out of doors in sunshine and rainstorms and in contact with boys who are poor and rich and of every variety" and that maybe she could do something with the Girl Scouts.

In the summer of 1933, with a daughter from Monroe's previous marriage, and their son, who was two at the time, the couple toured Germany with a group of Boy Scouts. Hotels were expensive. The group quickly swapped them for youth hostels. When the tour ended, Monroe escorted his young charges back to the USA, and then returned to join Isabel and the two children in Germany. Determined to find out more about youth hostels they met up with Richard Schirrmann.

He told them "many professors and many professional people, and a great number of learned enthusiasts who thought they could take hostelling to America… had all failed. They had come with neatly pressed suits and shiny glasses and notebooks." He had confidence in Isabel and Monroe because they were using youth hostels, wearing shorts, carrying knapsacks and riding bicycles. He thought they would succeed. He invited them to join the conference at Bad Godesberg.

The conference drew up a constitution and agreed contributions to a secretariat in Amsterdam but those at the conference were not ready to commit to a formal federation. Perhaps the presence of the Nazis unnerved them.

Ahead of the next international conference, Schirrmann travelled to France. He toured youth hostels for three weeks in the company of Marc Sangnier, the driving force behind youth hostels in France. At the first French youth hostel, at Bierville near Paris, Schirrmann unveiled a plaque, commemorating in big letters the names of Marc Sangnier, the founder, and Richard Schirrmann, the father of all the world's youth hostels.

Monroe Smith, having fulfilled Schirrmann's confident prediction by founding the American Youth Hostels Association, was back in Europe with some of the first American youth hostel members. He was photographed at the ceremony with Schirrmann.

The third international conference was held in England, in October 1934. The conference aimed to pool ideas, and to achieve greater freedom of travel for young people, as the threat of a second world war grew ever greater. Despite the Nazi take-over of youth hostels in Germany, Schirrmann attended with delegates from Belgium, Czechoslovakia, Danzig, England and Wales, France, Germany, Holland, the Irish Republic, Luxembourg, Northern Ireland, Poland, Scotland and Switzerland.

After a meeting in London and a visit to Downing Street Schirrmann and other delegates travelled north to the little village of Cromford, in Derbyshire. The station, with its small homely buildings, designed to echo the look of a French chateau, was a short walk up a narrow lane from Willersley Castle, a Methodist hotel and conference centre, where they met for the next three days. With an agenda of 60 pages, their work included admitting Danzig, Luxembourg and Rumania to membership of the federation. After two long sessions on Thursday, Friday was set aside for visiting youth hostels.

They went by bus to youth hostels at Chester and Maeshafn in Wales. They stopped at the youth hostel in Llangollen for lunch before continuing to Shrewsbury for tea. During the journey in mist and rain they sang to entertain themselves, which Schirrmann always enjoyed. A concert of folk music and a film about youth hostels in England and Wales, *Youth Hails Adventure*, entertained them that night. After a conference session on Saturday morning, they visited another youth hostel at nearby Hartington Hall, where Bonnie Prince Charlie was reputed to have spent the night on his march south.

Schirrmann planted a copper beech tree at Hartington as a symbol of the friendship of the youth of all nations. They visited the youth hostel at Derwent Hall and joined an informal dinner party of English members at Overton Hall. Afterwards they held an international social evening, playing traditional games and teaching each other their own countries' dances.

Some of the hostels they saw in England amused Schirrmann who had not expected to find youth hostels in grand mansions. "Though we have great hostels in Germany, we have not got the atmosphere of your wonderful Halls, which have a splendid tone and character of their own, due perhaps to the fact that they have been real homes where people have lived. Now indeed they are perfect homes for youth." On Sunday, following a final session, delegates climbed Black Rocks, a weathered outcrop of gritstone with panoramic views of the Derwent Valley.

Scotland and Ireland offered delegates tours after the conference. Schirrmann chose Ireland and, with eight others, visited every one of *An Óige's* youth hostels. Schirrmann planted an ash tree at Ireland's first youth hostel at Mellifont in the Boyne Valley. The charm and simplicity of *An Óige's* little hostels delighted him. He recognised that efforts and sacrifice had opened these little hostels which had none of the official support he had enjoyed in Germany. He did not judge hostels by the standard of comfort achieved but "by the way in which the youth hostel idea has been adapted to the special needs and character" of other countries.

Tensions in Germany had not emerged into or disrupted their meetings in England. The next year's conference in Cracow, Poland, passed equally well. After the conference the Smiths invited

Schirrmann to visit the United States.

In the USA, Isabel Smith anxiously encouraged Schirrmann to write out a speech he was due to give in Chicago, so that she could translate it for him. Schirrmann spoke no English. But when the passionate Schirrmann spoke he ignored his prepared words entirely. The audience applauded his emotional speech, Isabel recalled, though no more than four people understood a word he had said or realised how badly wrong her translation had gone.

Touring the States Schirrmann spoke to Rotary Clubs, women's organisations, universities and schools drumming up support for the Smiths and their work to bring his ideas to America. He urged more youth hostels in America and more travel for young people. American youth hostels in private houses reminded him again of the first youth hostels in Germany. A lunch with the First Lady, Eleanor Roosevelt, who spoke German, scheduled for half an hour lasted for two.

Monroe and Isabel Smith had invited Schirrmann to dedicate their first youth hostel at Northfield, Massachusetts.

Staying with the couple, Schirrmann opened the new youth hostel. It was in a chateau because, for Isabel, it was as close to the Castle Altena as any building in America. When he turned for home, Schirrmann had been away for more than two months and had travelled 10,000 miles.

On his return to Germany, the impact of the Nazis on youth hostels was increasingly plain. The reassuring house parents were gone. They now wore uniforms, were often party officials and the walls of hostels displayed Hitler's pictures. Individuals and small groups stopped wandering between youth hostels. Large uniformed groups of Hitler Youth, marching in step, singing political songs, replaced them.

The Nazis tolerated Schirrmann, perhaps for the esteem in which he was held outside Germany rather than for his importance within Germany. There is evidence of personal animosity towards Schirrmann and for his own equivocal relations with the Nazis. Certainly he continued as an honorary officer within Germany and outside Germany remained as president of the international movement.

The next international conference, in Copenhagen in 1936, was stormy. Disagreements caused long wrangles at the conference. Again the Nazis wanted German-speaking associations from neighbouring countries admitted to the federation. The Nazi delegates walked out, putting pressure on Schirrmann to resign too.

Despairing, Schirrmann feared their failures would break up the federation and make international youth travel impossible. Danish delegates presented him with honorary membership of the Danish Rambler's Guild. As the conference closed, Isabel Smith handed out roses as a symbol of peace to departing guests.

When the conference was done, Germany withdrew from the federation. They claimed the existing framework was frustrating their plans for a big expansion of the movement. In reality they left because their new German associations, in countries like Latvia and Rumania, had not been accepted.

Without a German presence in the international movement Schirrmann's position as president was untenable. If the sole purpose of Schirrmann for the Nazis was to retain contact and a position in the international movement, that purpose was now lost and Schirrmann himself had become irrelevant to youth hostels in Germany.

*4. Isabel and Monroe Smith, founders of the American
Youth Hostels Association*

Fruitfulness

In July 1937 Schirrmann finally gave in. He resigned as president of the international federation and gave up any role in German youth hostels. Aged 63 Schirrmann retreated to the Taunus Hills, to Grävenwiesbach among cornfields and apple orchards. There, he was almost back where he had been in 1903 when his marriage had been failing and when the head teacher of his school had refused permission for him to take pupils on wandering expeditions away from the classroom.

This time he could not transfer to a more sympathetic school but he was no longer alone. In 1929 his shadow marriage had finally ended and he had married his much younger secretary, Elisabeth Bordeck. Their marriage was happy. Elisabeth shared his ideas and supported his work. They would eventually have six children. Surrounded by a growing family in Grävenwiesbach, Schirrmann lived on his modest teacher's pension on a small holding in a lifestyle familiar from childhood.

His ideas had taken root beyond German borders. The original ideas of youth hostels, despite the Nazi effort, were at least preserved outside their founding country. Without him, his old friends at the conference of 1938 elected Jack Catchpool as president in his place.

Catchpool was an inspired and fortunate choice. He had been instrumental in transplanting the idea of youth hostels to Britain. A Quaker, he was an enthusiastic internationalist. He had travelled widely during the first world war, in Russia, the Far East and in Palestine. He was also a strong supporter of voluntarism having come to youth hostels from voluntary social service in the East End of London.

Briefly, Schirrmann remained in touch. After the conference in 1938, Terry Trench of *An Óige* personally delivered a farewell message from the conference to Schirrmann. Trench found Schirrmann supplementing his small teacher's pension by growing fruit and vegetables at Grävenwiesbach.

Catchpool's colleague, Graham Heath, visited Schirrmann in August 1939. He described Schirrmann as an extraordinarily boy-like man of 65 in a house full of young children. Frau Schirrmann served Heath a meal and the two men talked about youth hostels, in Germany and abroad, before Heath left, promising to take messages to Schirrmann's friends in other countries.

Schirrmann feared that he would not see his friends again for a long time. War began the next month. Whilst the Nazis overran the rest of Europe, Catchpool resolutely maintained and developed

Schirrmann's ideas in England, one of the few European countries the Nazis had not invaded.

Youth hostels in England and Wales prospered. By the end of the war they were stronger than they had been at the start. Catchpool gained official support for youth hostels in Britain and kept in touch with associations out of Europe. At the invitation of Isabel and Monroe Smith, Catchpool's family, except for his eldest daughter, spent the war in Massachusetts, where his wife, Ruth, ran the youth hostel in Northfield.

War brought a lessening of pressure on Schirrmann from the Nazis. Too busy with their battles they forgot their feud with him. He resumed teaching. He was able to go wandering again with his pupils though he found the countryside deserted with "no sign of anyone on foot… no youth groups." Schools had given up walking and other teachers found Schirrmann strange; a man of his age, wandering with a blanket, kettle, pans and a knapsack. The old free and easy spirit of walking from hostel to hostel, of the *Wandervogel*, was gone. In 1944 he celebrated his 70th birthday with Münker and other old friends at Altena Castle.

As the war ended in 1945, the indomitable Schirrmann began working to bring youth hostels back to life. He, Münker and others set about contacting one another in a country overwhelmed with refugees, occupied and divided by invaders. German youth hostels had been devastated. Out of 1,130 hostels, in the three zones of Germany occupied by the Allies, only 630 still existed. Allied forces regarded youth hostels with suspicion, because of their links with the Nazis. They requisitioned most of those that had not been bombed or destroyed.

RICHARD SCHIRRMANN

In 1946 Monroe Smith arrived in Europe on the troop ship, *Ernie Pyle*, loaded with youth hostel members, "and ten tons of lumber, glass, hammers, nails, putty, etc plus food for the entire summer, bicycles and sleeping bags..." They rebuilt bombed youth hostels in France, Belgium, Holland, Luxembourg and Germany. Monroe toured Germany with Schirrmann and then he arranged for Schirrmann and Münker to travel, without visas or passports, to Scotland. At Loch Lomond youth hostel in September, a year after war ended, the first international conference since 1938 was held.

The visitors from Germany provoked interest. Schirrmann was as charismatic as ever. At a youth rally before the conference started, young people thronged to join Schirrmann, keen to see more of the man who invented hostels. He led singing, played games and signed books.

Not everyone was ready to welcome him. Some at the conference had served as soldiers or in the resistance. "I cannot endure the sound of the German language," one delegate, who had been in a concentration camp, announced.

The conference agreed with the Czechoslovakians "no help should be given to those countries responsible for the war, before considering the just claims of their victims." Representing Germany at the meeting, Schirrmann pleaded for recognition of youth hostels in his country but on the application for German membership the conference made no decision. The move on behalf of Germany in any event was premature. No official organisation existed yet in Germany.

Work continued to restore youth hostels in Germany. Always an optimist, remembering only the welcome young people had given him and ignoring the terrible circumstances of Germany, Schirrmann set up a youth hostel in a barn in Grävenwiesbach. He pressed for a more permanent arrangement. He was used to obstacles. He had lived through shortages of money and materials in the aftermath of a previous world war.

Against the wishes of the federation, Jack Catchpool arrived in Hamburg in 1947 with a working party to help restore youth hostels. They worked alongside young Germans, repairing and adapting a former barracks to youth hostel use.

Schirrmann travelled to the 1948 international conference in Ireland at Kilbride youth hostel in a disused army camp in the Wicklow hills, south of Dublin. Hundreds climbed to the summit of Seefin with its views west across the Wicklow Hills. Young people from the former enemy countries surrounded Schirrmann on the summit. "His youthful enthusiasm and his ability to communicate with young people of every nationality, though he spoke and understood no language but German" captivated them.

Efforts to rebuild youth hostels in Germany triumphed again. In October 1949 a national youth hostel organisation was established in the three western occupation zones. In a ceremony at Altena Castle Schirrmann took an honorary position. The president of the German Federal Republic sent congratulations, recognizing Schirrmann's life's work.

In 1957, aged 83, Schirrmann attended celebrations for the 25th anniversary of the international federation, back in Amsterdam where the federation had been born. He continued to be fitter than many younger men. He came from sturdy country folk, had been abstemious all his life, had taken a cold bath every morning, and was still a strong walker though his eyesight was failing.

In autumn 1961 he fell seriously ill. Transferred to hospital in Frankfurt he passed away on 14 December. He was 87 years old. Münker declared that the many old friends, attending his funeral at Altena, had come to accompany him on his last wandering.

Monroe and Isabel Smith left the American Youth Hostels Association in 1949 to found Youth Argosy, a travel company organising charter flights for young people between the USA and Europe. Isabel's art filled the pages of the American Youth Hostels' magazine, *Knapsack*.

Jack Catchpool retired as president of the international federation in 1950 but he continued his work with youth hostels informally, and unofficially in countries around the world.

Graham Heath, who had visited Schirrmann at Grävenwiesbach, in August 1939, became secretary-general of the international youth hostel federation and went on to write a biography of Richard Schirrmann.

5. International youth hostels meeting at Willersley Castle, Derbyshire, 1934. Richard Schirrmann front row, fifth from left, with Jack Catchpool to his right and Heer Deelen to his left.

Postscript

Richard Schirrmann believed nothing was too good for youth. Even in old age he loved spending time with young people. He focused his energy and his life's work on young people, and what was best for them. He put young people first and that, more than anything, should be his legacy. He loved the company of young people.

He inspired adults. He cajoled and encouraged until eventually his ideas took root. He enlisted the support of others throughout his life. He deserved the praise, awards, and commendations he received. Nothing was inevitable about his ideas. He worked. He worked hard. He persisted, and despite setbacks, he inspired others.

He emerged from a time that was waiting for youth hostels. His ideas came from a wider movement, of *Wandervogel*, of a drive to get back to the countryside. Germany was ripe for youth hostels as the 19th century became the 20th. Other countries were ready for youth hostels in the aftermath of the 1914-18 war. His idea took root in already prepared and fertile ground.

Youth hostels were ready and waiting when young people burst into world wide travel, from the 1950s onward. His ideas found a new, international audience. Now we are all travelling, now we are all holiday makers, his idea offers something simple, authentic and communal that appeals to many still. His invention has prospered and endured.

Today there are at least 4,000 official youth hostels in 90 countries around the world and the independent hostel booking web site, *Hostel World*, lists 35,000 hostels in 180 countries. Richard Schirrmann inspired them all.

6.Richard and Elisabeth Schirrmann and family

Notes and References

I began research into Richard Schirrmann's life while I was investigating the development of youth hostels in England and Wales and the people and ideas behind them. When I came to revise the manuscript for that book, I cut large pieces of text relating to Richard Schirrmann. His youth hostels inspired the development of youth hostels in Britain but frustratingly his story did not fit easily into the story of youth hostels in England and Wales. Loath to see all the research I had done go to waste, I decided to develop this book.

I made wide use of the YHA (England and Wales) public archives in the Special Collections, Cadbury Research Library, University of Birmingham.

p30   "Though we have…" Derbyshire Countryside Magazine,
       January 1953, p23
p30   "by the way…" Trench, Fifty Years Young, p52

Chapter Five - Fruitfulness.

p37   "no sign…" from Heath, Richard Schirrmann, p52
p38   "and ten tons of lumber…" from Smith, Isabel Bacheler
       Smith, p225
p38   "I cannot endure the sound of the German language…"
       from Grassl, Heath, The Magic Triangle, p90
p38   "no help should be given to those countries…" ibid p90
p39   "His youthful enthusiasm and his ability…" from Trench,
       Fifty Years Young.

Acknowledgements

I've been involved with youth hostels for many years. Passing questions, brief chats and conversations in bars, hostel lounges or out walking fuelled my interest in Richard Schirrmann.

More people than I can remember have helped or contributed to this book, in Britain, Europe, and throughout the world wherever there are youth hostels. Many people asked questions or offered information over many years. For the friendship and support they have all shown I am grateful.

I could not have written this book without Graham Heath's biography of Richard Schirrmann. I have used his book extensively, adding other information I have gained from wider research into youth hostels in England and Wales.

Heath's books are out of print, which partly prompted this small book. His books sometimes become available, second-hand in bookshops or on line. They're available in the YHA Archive, in the Cadbury Research Library - Special Collections, the University of Birmingham. I am indebted to Graham Heath.

Acknowledgements

Isabel and Monroe Smith came to my attention for the part they played in various international conferences, particularly the story of Isabel handing out red roses at the end of the Copenhagen conference in 1936. I am grateful to Daniel Smith for recording the wider story of their involvement in youth hostels in the USA and Europe. He generously supplied images and allowed the full use of his biography of Isabel.

I am extremely grateful to John Martin, YHA's honorary archivist, for his constant supply of enthusiasm, information and the images he unearths from the unlikeliest of places.

As ever, thanks to my wife, Caroline, for her tolerance, support, and encouragement, without which this book would have neither begun nor ended.

Bibliography

Catchpool, E St John, Candles in the Darkness, the Bannisdale Press, London, 1966

Coburn, Oliver, The Youth Hostel Story, the first twenty years in England and Wales, The National Council of Social Service, London 1950

Grassl, Anton, and Heath, Graham, The Magic Triangle, a short history of the world youth hostel movement, IYHF 1982

Heath, Graham, Richard Schirrmann, the first youth hosteller, A biographical sketch, International Youth Hostel Federation, Copenhagen, 1962

Smith, Daniel, Isabel Bacheler Smith: Artist, Teacher, Mother, & Peacemaker, Living Legacy Productions, 2012

Stachura, The German Youth Movement 1900 – 1945

Trench, Terry, Fifty Years Young, the story of An Óige, Irish Youth Hostels Association, Dublin, 1981

Biesanz, John, Nazi influences on German Youth Hostels, Social Forces Vol 19 No 4, May 1941

Youth and Peace, Derbyshire Countryside Magazine, January 1953

Index

DUNCAN M SIMPSON

Open To All

How Youth Hostels Changed the World

Youth hostels changed the world. Beginning in 1929 with no money, no leader and only a simple idea, today they boast bars, restaurants and en suites. You can find them in cities, in towns, in the wilderness, in castles, mansions, mills and converted hotels.

"A fascinating account of the history of the YHA, beautifully written..."

"enjoyable, accessible... a "must have" for anyone with more than a passing interest in YHA..."

"a truly impressive piece of research with detailed biographies of the key players involved in this fabulous institution that has given so much pleasure to so many of us."

"Interwoven with the history is Duncan's own story of working for YHA."

www.duncanmsimpsonwriting.com

Printed in Great Britain
by Amazon